POETIC PRESCRIPTIONS FOR ETERNAL YOUTH

EXAMINING EARTHLY BEAUTY FROM A HEAVENLY PERSPECTIVE

KATHERINE NORLAND

Poetic Prescriptions Publishing
PO Box 17033
Encino, CA 91416

Photos and cover art by RT Norland
www.RobertNorland.com

Other books by the author:

Poetic Prescriptions for Plaguing Problems: Biblical Remedies for When Life Bites

Poetic Prescriptions for Pesky Problems

For more information, please visit www.PoeticPrescriptions.com.

The 2 Corinthians 4:7 scripture quoted in the preface is from the King James Version (KJV). All other references to scripture are paraphrased from various versions of the Holy Bible.

POETIC PRESCRIPTIONS FOR ETERNAL YOUTH

EXAMINING EARTHLY BEAUTY FROM A HEAVENLY PERSPECTIVE

KATHERINE NORLAND

Dedication

To all the exquisite souls in the world who live each day to be an example, who sacrifice to help their fellow man, who put aside their infatuation with themselves and use their gifts and their talents to make a difference for others. For all those who keep shining even when they're asked to dim their light. For all those who are beautifully scarred from fighting the battle while trying to leave this world better than they found it.

To my husband, Rob, who keeps me grounded. To my son, Timothy, who helps me keep my sense of humor.

To Timothy Oman, who helps me think outside the box.

To Darlene, my cheerleader, my biggest fan, and my mentor.

To my late friend Marshall, who convinced me to dust off my poetry and put it out into the world because it was needed and worth reading.

Contents

Preface

Is it just me, or do you also remember words spoken to you about your appearance all the way back to your childhood, like a cracker you secretly put in your pocket to save for later and forgot about, now smashed into little pieces that you don't know are there until you sit down and bits of it fall out of your pocket? Or each time you reach into your pocket and pull your hand back out, you've got crumbs embedded in your fingernails.

You've tried to turn those pockets inside out and shake away that debris, but those little word crumbs leave trails into your consciousness and attract other vermin to eat the scraps. Whether those words were spoken from well-meaning relatives, lovers, or peers, something about them stuck, and not only do they seem impossible to get rid of (even with the best lint roller), but it also seems like those opinions are the absolute truth.

And that hurts the most.

Personally, I've heard hundreds of disparaging remarks, maybe thousands. I've had lots of crackers crumble in my pockets over the years.

More than a decade or two later, I can remember being told crunchy words like: "You're too pretty to be that fat." "You look like a circus freak." "Is that acne or do you have meningitis?" "A woman's face should not be that hairy." "You have a blonde beard." "You're not smart enough to do that." "You're not going to succeed." "You're too pale." "You're husky." "You're not fat; you're just thick." "Those lines on your neck make you look 10 years older than your face does." "If you want to get work in this business, you've really got to fix your teeth." "Your lips are too thin; you need to get collagen." "You would be pretty, but you look like you're from Nebraska."

What did that last one even mean?

I had such an unhealthy self-esteem and misshapen view of myself that I could literally bring myself to tears just by looking in the mirror—though the mirror never involuntarily cracked when I looked in it...

I believed that I was hideous, disgusting, and not worth the dirt that I was made out of.

It really didn't matter if those crummy words were spoken by friends, enemies, or frenemies. What mattered was that I chose to believe them. I ate them all up until they destroyed me. I not only let them take up residence in my mind but I also let them stop me from pursuing my dreams, taking risks, wearing sleeveless shirts on hot summer days, and getting my picture taken with loved ones (if I did, I would hide in the back row so you couldn't see all of me).

I let others' remarks stifle my life for far too long.

Then, as if God couldn't have given someone a more difficult calling or desire based on how they saw themselves, I felt compelled to move to Hollywood and become an actress.

I, this heinous creature who couldn't stand my own sight, would now pursue a profession where all of my flaws—every pound and pore—would be blown up on the big screen and magnified. I would be in competition for roles against all the most gorgeous people in the world, who were told, "You should be an actress or a model." In my Minnesota coveralls and thick sweaters, with yellow teeth in need of braces, I wandered into the epicenter of breathtaking beauty, with nothing but a Chevy full of my belongings and a pocket full of chocolate (still covered in cracker crumbs).

I remember when I first moved to Hollywood and I sat awkwardly in an audition waiting room looking at these Barbie dolls that wore size zero. Zero?! I thought they were kidding when they said zero.

My smallest friend in high school was a size four. I thought just being in the single digits was a feat in itself. When my little size-four friend got out of high school and got pregnant, she actually had the nerve to ask me if she could borrow some of my clothes for a few months because she didn't want to buy maternity clothes!

Then, she proudly told me after she had the baby, that she didn't know what happened but now she was going to have to buy new clothes after all, because she was even smaller now than before she got pregnant, and her clothes were too big! Ugh, some people's genes.

Back to that audition and the size zeros. I didn't even know that zero was a size, and wanting so desperately to fit in and make friends, I foolishly proclaimed, "I'm a perfect 10." Size 10. They snickered, laughed, and let me know that when people speak of being a "perfect 10," they are definitely not talking about clothing size!

And once again I felt like I didn't have what it took, or the body I needed, to do what I loved, to follow my dreams.

But I also knew there was no way I was going to starve myself to fulfill my dreams. I had two friends in high school with eating disorders, one with anorexia and the other with bulimia. I didn't have the will power to limit my food consumption; quite the opposite, I could eat more than a full-grown man. This chick likes big portions. I tried once or twice to throw up, but it was far too time consuming, stinky, and unpleasant. I wasn't organized enough, like my friend, to carry toothpaste, mouthwash, and boxes of mints.

In my short-lived experiment, I found that it burns more on the way up than on the way down. Plus, I heard that it rotted your teeth, and I didn't want my teeth to look any worse than they already did.

So I had to start eating more fruits and veggies and get rid of junk food. Does switching to organic junk food count? Let's pretend for a moment it does.

Turns out that eating half of a large meat-lovers, cheese-stuffed-crust pizza for dinner, followed by an entire pumpkin pie (after the only fruit you've had for breakfast came in the form of cherry pie filling in the six or seven donuts you consumed) is not a recommended health plan from any dietitian. Who woulda thunk?

Have you ever heard the phrase, "It's what's on the inside that counts"? I've not only heard it but I've also said it and I believe it. Well, I believed it only when it came to other people, not me.

It's odd that we can overlook the most glaring physical flaws in another, while at the same time magnifying the minuscule ones in ourselves. We compare the worst in ourselves to the best in others. We pine over their perfect butt and despise our wobbly bits.

By now you may be wondering how I got over my self-loathing. It took a while, and it certainly wasn't from anyone I knew giving me compliments or telling me I looked better than I thought I did or that there was nothing wrong with me.

The way I moved past it was by studying what the God who actually created me had to say about His workmanship. The following verses are paraphrased from the Bible scriptures below.

I am fearfully and wonderfully made (Psalm 139:14); my grey hair is a crown of glory (Proverbs 16:31); man looks at outward appearance but God looks at the heart (1 Samuel 16:7); beauty is fleeting, but a woman who fears the Lord should be praised (Proverbs 31:30); beauty shouldn't come from outward adornment; the unfading beauty is a gentle and quiet spirit (1 Peter 3:3-4); we were created in God's own image (Genesis 1:27); and God formed us from dust and breathed life into us (Genesis 2:7).

I could say something about each one of these scriptures, but for me, the one that really cracked my mirror (in a good way) was 2 Corinthians 4:7: "But we have this treasure in earthen vessels, that the excellency of the power may be of God, and not of us"...

Wait, what? We are not these dust buckets we live in? It's just a place where our treasure hides? A place where we and the Holy Spirit reside?

And then I got to thinking that those of us with the most cracks in our jars of clay can often be a better testament to the power and greatness of God because He can shine through all of those cracks.

Perhaps people can see God even better when they are not distracted by our perfect symmetry, lest people think that what we accomplish in life is due to our good looks, and not the grace, favor, and blessings of God.

Letting the truth of God's word pervade gave me a check-up from the neck up and a much-needed makeover of the mind.

I was able to stop connecting who I am to the shell that I live in. My getting told at auditions that I'm too short, tall, fat, pale, etc., no longer became an issue of my worth. I just wasn't what they were looking for; they wanted a two-story house or a rambler, maybe a tiny house, or one with a tan exterior. I just wasn't right for that job. And when there was a job calling for a white, double-wide trailer, I'd get my shot.

I got to a place that when people put me down, I didn't crumble.

I found I was now able to separate what they said about my exterior from who I was, the same way we know that the house we live in isn't us.

Whether we live in a mansion or an RV, it doesn't have to define us, because it's not us. We are not our size (of course, we can make healthier eating choices for the sake of being on this earth disease-free long enough to carry out the mission God put us here for), but letting our size keep us from finding joy in our daily life is no longer acceptable.

Being upset about our skin color, moles, freckles, texture of our hair, or the length of our torso does us no good because those are little things that we have no control over. And if you can't do anything about it, why let it take up valuable real estate in your mind? If we're not able to do the little things, why be anxious about the rest? (Luke 12:26).

Sure, I wear make-up, get highlights in my hair, wear push-up bras, heels, have tried peels and facial injections a couple of times, and sometimes use one of those stretchy, tight encasings under my clothes to suck my gut in. I even took to heart one of those previous comments someone gave me, and fixed my teeth.

But bashing my head against the wall because the colors of my eyes don't match is no longer worth my valuable time.

There are billions of different versions of beauty, just as there are billions of people in the world. We've many preferences for what we think is hot or not. We have many schools of thought about whether it's okay to have cosmetic surgery, or even whether we should wear make-up, show our hair, expose our knees; heck, in some religions, only the eyes and hands are acceptable to display in public.

The poems and prose in this book aren't about whether fixing yourself up is okay or not. This is a book about finding out who you really are, accepting and loving yourself, knowing what God thinks about you, your true identity, and what's really important.

After all, 100 years from now, is what we looked like going to matter? Or is our legacy going to be the thing we are remembered for? Let's make that be the case.

It doesn't matter if you're pro or con on the plastic surgery debate. It doesn't matter whether you wore skirts down to your ankles. It doesn't matter that your virgin hair has never been colored. It doesn't even matter that, simply for beauty's sake, you've been poked more than a pin cushion.

What matters is how you lived your life.

Did you follow your calling? Did you live life to the fullest? Did you enjoy the body God gave you? Did you sacrifice your time in service of others? If the only thing people remember about you is that you had "work done," or looked great in a pair of jeans, then you haven't made the contribution to this world that needs to be made, that only you are capable of making.

So let us get the focus off ourselves. Let us get the focus off our flaws. Let us look to find ways that we can serve the world, which is in desperate need of help, and ask ourselves: How can I use my gifts, talents, money, ideas, and compassion to aid a fallen world and point the people in it to the God who answers all?

Introduction

I've had issues about the way I look since as far back as I can remember. There was a constant mantra running through my head that I was not good enough, smart enough, thin enough, or pretty enough. And let's face it: I was downright ugly.

That is how I saw myself.

How I thought about myself manifested in everything I did, and in the things I was too scared to even attempt to do. Feeling like you're the ugliest person in the room has its way of putting a chokehold on your life so you never step up and try new things. I couldn't raise my hand in class to answer a question; I feared that everyone would look at me and be able to see all the things I hated about myself.

The real problem wasn't how I actually looked, but how I saw myself.

Once I was able to change that, a whole new world of possibilities opened up for me. I found comfort in my own skin; I was unfazed by how I looked and what others thought of me. I was now free to run wholeheartedly after the dreams that I had previously been afraid to even begin.

My hope is that the poems and prose in this book take you on a journey, and that by reading about my ups and downs, you can also experience the same freedom of not just tolerating yourself, but loving yourself right where you are, moving past self-acceptance to a life focused on the bigger picture and being of contribution to others.

I broke this book up into three sections: The Before, The Plateau, and The After. Like most transformations one goes through, there are stages; it usually doesn't happen overnight or in an instant.

In **The Before**, you've got the snapshot of what your life looks like. Whether we are talking about your physical appearance, how you behave, or what you know to be true, there is your way of being before you knew what you now know, sometimes even before you knew that there was something in need of change.

But you're restless, unsure, not comfortable in your own skin; longing to look like or be like someone you admire, someone who seems to have a perfect life, body, career, spouse; but you thought you didn't have what it took to get those things or be like that person.

But then something inside you insisted that this isn't all there is; there is more; you can do more, be more, and have more than what you've got now, which sends you on the journey of seeking out The After you desire.

Then comes **The Plateau**. You realized a change was needed, and you've started making progress.

You're not the person you once were. You now head towards your goals with more focus because you decided there is a better life you could be living. Your mind is set that from now on things are going to be different. You're thankful for the steps you've taken and how far you've come.

But then something trips you up; you get stuck. You stop making progress, possibly even slip back further. Perhaps it's from old habits or ways of being, a lack of clarity about how you need to get where you're going.

Or could it be your perception of yourself and your circumstances? You're still not able to see yourself as worthy of attaining your goal, and that could be the unseen plateau that stops you from reaching The After. The only way you can get unstuck is by figuring out how to break the plateau, which is by knowing the truth of who you are and whose you are.

In **The After**, you've made your transformation! You may not be what others consider picture-perfect, but you know you're a different person than when you began, and that nothing about the way you look can keep you from your destiny. And this "after" snapshot has far more to do with your outlook than the way you look on the outside. Knowing the truth about yourself will do far more for your life than will fitting into your jeans from high school.

You now accept yourself for who you are, whether you've gotten the desired physical changes or not, because you now know with all certainly that you are not the skin you're in.

You are an infinite being that will go on living long after this body of yours drops back into the dust. And when your mind is no longer caught up on the inevitability of fading youth, you can go on without hindrance and make the biggest difference in the areas you care about and with the people whose lives you long to touch.

So follow me while I shatter the misconceptions about our looks—and let's go from head to toe and discover our true identity.

The Before

Ode to the Zit Queen

I hate the way I look,
Though some would call me blessed.
When I add up my book,
I never pass the test.
I know that you're in awe
With Acne Vulgaris.
I only see each flaw;
I fall into these pits.

I tried suppressing it,
Used tonics for each pimple,
Must pop each nasty zit;
You think it'd be more simple.
Don't wanna sing the blues
Over superficial things
When many have deep issues
And not just surface dings.

I'm called to do a craft
With close-ups of my face.
In*cyst* I need skin graft;
Outbreaks can't be erased.
I've got potholes for pores,
Red marks and acne scars.
Zits pop up all the more
Like peanut shells in bars.

A "beauty mark," I say,
This Mount Vesuvius,
With face concealed in clay,

Their answers dubious.
Oil slicks have spent my rent;
Cures tried but none have worked.
Lost every stinkin' cent
Being poked until I hurt.

But I can't leave my bed
If I leave zits alone.
I've hundreds of whiteheads
And polka dot skin tone.
I can't look in the mirror
Still loathing what I see.
Until my skin is clearer
I don't want to be me.

It's true, a perfect glow
Won't heal this blemished world.
I know that comedo
Made my emotions hurl.
What sends me in a whirl
Is wanting spots' removal.
Deep down I'm still that girl
Who's searching for approval.

Boobies!

Why is it some are so obsessed?
Goodness, it's just a female breast!
Yet I admit, I've been a bit
Concerned when getting dressed.
Half-empty cups are no hope chest;
I couldn't get a dress to fit.
Wide hips and butt would make seams pop
If I had bought for size on top.

No hour glass, what could I do?
So separates bought was all I knew.
The tops I got were always smaller
Shown by the tag, a size or two.
Since then, I'm thankful that I grew.
In junior high, torment I'd holler
Bullied by pubescent teens
They'd say I was a Pirate's Dream...

And yes, by now you may have guessed
That meant I had a sunken chest.
With cutting jokes I was replete;
In wonder bras I would invest,
With extra pads to look my best.
They asked if I did not have feet
Would I still need support from shoes.
Well...no. "Then why wear bras?!" they booed.

Those thoughtless teens can be so mean,
Like when they called me "Carpenter's Dream:

Flat as a board, easy to nail."
So much for healthy self-esteem!
This bloomer-late no longer screams,
But busty gals, they soon will rail.
Now having small boobs not a drag
'Cause to my knees they'll never sag!

Butt of the Jokes

I don't know what is wrong with me;
Oh, Lord, I wish I knew.
I always do the opposite
Of what's deemed right to do.

When given opportunities,
I stay here, stuck in fear
Of others and how they'll react;
The insults I might hear.

You say that I should guard my heart;
I try; I really do.
But I allow what others think
To stick to me like glue.

Their syrup-words do not taste sweet;
In tacky mess I stay.
Wish I could block the negative
From what these people say.

Before I let it travel 'round
I want to knock it to the ground,
To block my ears ahead of time
To anything that's not sublime.

But even those whom I hold dear
Say tough things I don't want to hear.
Lock up their lips to make them stop.
A wordsmith cop should guard my block!
They poke and prod, make fun of me;

I feel it's done deliberately.
It stinks to be the butt of jokes;
My redness is from all their pokes.

"Where is your humor? It's a joke.
Don't swallow it; you just might choke.
Calm down; there's no need to act out."
"Then don't make fun of me!" I shout.

Don't get me wrong; I love some puns;
Not aimed at me, I guide.
I promise that a knock-knock joke
Would surely split my side.

Oh, God, help me so I can see
It's not me they attack,
That when they call me out in jest,
I'm not knifed in the back.

So help me laugh and not feel hurt
No matter what they seem to blurt.
When they come at me with a slam,
Don't let me question who I am.

Perhaps I must change how I see,
That it's not them... it could be me.
For they're not who I truly duel;
It's to myself that I've been cruel.

If laughter is a medicine
Please fill up my prescription,

And send me each *Laugh At Yourself*
Magazine subscription.

If sensitive to others' jokes,
There's something underneath they poke.
Until that's fixed, I'll never be
At peace, or able to be free.

Busti-ego

Wearing an ensemble fit only for a runway walk, my alter ego swished into the room. And she, plus-sized in all her purgatory, busted out from every seam. She worked a midriff jewel-encrusted satin busti-ego, with push-up psyche. She donned a far-too-short self with a waistline several inches below her inner nature.

Having thrown herself onto the chair, she laughed gregariously, then kicked her feet up on a coffee table not meant for spiked heels. I marveled at her confidence, her self-assuredness and carefree attitude.

If I were to wear a midriff top, I'd stay standing in the corner, arms folded, covering my pasty gut, at the very least sucking it in each time I heard someone come near, for fear they would happen to see me.

But she, she didn't care! Her Rubenesque, soft-flesh stomach hung out above her mini skirt; she was unashamed of her muffintop. Nothing in the least seemed to bother her.

She indulged in creamy, long, glazed split donuts filled with Bavarian cream, and drizzled with chocolate. She asked no permission and made no apologies as she dove for a second one.

There's a story I heard once: When the wealthier dieting ladies on the Titanic were asked of any regrets, they said they wished they hadn't skipped dessert.

Could it really ever be possible that I could be that comfortable beneath my own skin?

Years later I would come to recognize this encasing wasn't me at all. It was just the current house I lived in. And maybe it shouldn't bother me if it needs a little maintenance. The true me dwells inside, just waiting to come out, wanting to fly through the air and dance through the clouds, dying to shed this domicile that weighs me down so much.

Yes, life is short. I'll love myself, as I am, for all that I am and all that I am not. I'll not feel the need to conform, or even to suck my psyche in. Now please, alter ego, save a donut for me!

HATE

Hate, hate is all I see;
Each mirror in the world hates me.

"H" is for the headache
I gave to everyone.
"A" is for gigantic ass
I made of me when done.
"T" is for the trouble
I done put people through.
"E" is for each little thing
That's bad that I've done too.

No multitudes of words
That are encouragin'
Will change the fact this face
Could use a plastic "suragin'."

I'm good at hiding me,
For that'd be when I'm at my best.
Just ask me how I feel;
I'll tell you well, and pass the test.

"H" is for the heavy load
That I am called to carry.
"A" is for anxiety
That I alone must bury.
"T" is for the tedious time
I've spent alone, unknown.
"E" is for excruciating,
The cage I'm bound in when at home.

Can anyone proceed
To look at me and hold their laugh?
I'm let down by each shrink
They've made me speak to on the staff.

I hide behind facades,
My make-up, coiffed hair, and my clothes.
But when I write, I leak,
Releasing what nobody knows.

"H" is for the harshest harm
That I've inflicted onto me.
"A" is for the attitude
That I've displayed for all to see.
"T" is for tremendous tons
I tip the scales with all this weight.
"E" is for the eyesore,
My faulty face that seals my fate.

Hate! Hate! It's all I see;
I hate you 'cause I first hate me!

So What? We All Get Old

So what? We all get old.
That's just the way it goes.
There're billions being spent
To stop the aging show.
But if we fix our face,
The next step is our neck.
We race against the clock;
Our hands have gone to heck.

"Don't let me age one bit,"
Sometimes I often beg.
My sexy six-pack gone
And now I sport a keg?
Poor workouts, junky food,
Could it be age and stress?
My hips could hide beneath
An antebellum dress.

No matter what I do,
This waist I cannot whittle.
I dread the spread to come
Called menopausal middle.
"I can't wear tank tops now;
I've bingo wings!" I moan.
Look at my flabby arms;
They once had so much tone.

I fought a fearsome fight
In the 'Furniture Wars.'
Ol' grav'ty took my chest

And dropped it in my drawers.
My perky butt is gone,
Not smooth and round and high,
But bags of cottage cheese
That slap against my thighs.

"Enough!" I say, "This hurts!"
Now I'm an angry pouter.
My thighs have gotten chaffed.
Where is that talcum powder?
My hair thins on my head
And grows thick on my chin.
My hormones are a wreck.
What monster's in my skin?

I've got some new disease,
If wrinkles weren't enough,
They call it C.R.S.
For, Can't Remember...Stuff.
I reminisce with pics;
How nice I once was stacked.
Kids ask me if I'm broken;
With spider veins I'm cracked.

Can't I embrace this state?
There's not much I can do
But live the best I can
And be a blessing too.
So what? We all get old.
I focus on what matters,
What touches others' lives,
Not that I've gotten fatter.

If I have lived my call
Exchanged my life for His
It's immaterial
What size my casket is.

The Plateau

Eternal Youth

Once radiant and dewy skin
Now flaky, with the dullest hue.
Are answers in light therapy
To make old faces like mine new?

Plump visitors have left my face
But they forgot to take their bags.
My skin has sunken in, now thin,
Like paper-crepe in wind, it wags.

My eyes, once dove-like, looked so sweet
Till crows flew 'way, but left their feet.
Eternal youth through fingers slip;
Our time on earth is but a blip.

New fillers, or old collagen?
Both will wear off, and so, what then?
Wished looking great could be more subtle;
Ask friends for tips in girl-time huddle.

Those men with age look more distinguished;
To be a man's not what I wish!
Now compliments go to my brother,
And in the mirror I see mother.

Some folks will do 'most anything;
To keep what's left of youth, they'll cling.
But I'd at 80 be a joke
If looking 30 when I croak.

Say "Yes" to Jesus and you'll gain
A youngness that your age can't change.
With God doth come sound surgery
Where youth's obtained eternally.

Shut My Shortcake Hole

I embody moderation. Yeah, right!
It's in the portions that I lack control.
Wish I could wait for them to bake, not eat
The whole big bowl of snickerdoodle dough!

Instead of this fat-laden treat
That just expands my growing gut,
I need to dine on God's sweet Word
And keep my greedy pie hole shut.

I hate that I've insatiable desires;
Just wiped my breakfast mouth, now dream of
lunch.
I don't as often think of time for prayer.
I need a date with God, not Nestlè Crunch.

I worry more 'bout fitting in
My daily meals, desserts, and snacks
Than hearing perfect wisdom on
Preventing all these flesh attacks.

How can I crave God's Word as much
As a tantalizing gourmet spread?
Instead of shortcake, I must make
The Word of God my daily bread.

My Bible's read, yet when the book is closed,
I relish kettles of my cankered sin.
I retch on precepts that I should ingest.
Instead prefer the road-kill where I've been.

If I'd been gorging on the good from God
The way I do with Mom's cheese casserole
My appetite would be in my control,
Led by the Lord, and not my shortcake hole.

House of Mirrors

When entering the house of mirrors, I carried every bag collected over my lifetime. These bags were filled with every label, every name I'd been called, every remark ever said about who I am. It took countless trips to carry all my bags inside. There was no end. I couldn't fit through the door, initially, and then it was only me to infinity.

Every surface reflected me. I could see from every angle. I looked curved, deformed, and mangled. It was shocking. I was startled at the number of bags I was holding and how worn I looked from lugging them around. I clutched them tighter. No sooner had I entered and saw the stark reality of who I was than I immediately got lost. I couldn't see where to turn. The only thing inside was reflective glass everywhere...and me—me and my bags in all directions. I was uncomfortable. I didn't want to confront the images, yet this ghostly luggage and those piercing stares begged introspection.

But how could I look inside when my outside begged my attention?

Whispers of jeers pushed themselves out of those bags I lugged. Cat calls at my psyche, "You're not good enough, smart enough, thin enough, young enough," wafted from those open bags. I bolted up and ran around while trying to close their mouths. From bag to bag I did my best to seal them shut. I twisted, I clipped, I tied and knotted. I went from bag to bag to bag, distressed from the haunting words of my past that, like a ball and chain, I chose to keep and carry.

I collapsed on those piles of trash and fell out, exhausted. The long-buried contents escaped and began to suffocate me. I wanted to disappear. I leaped up and looked for a passageway out. But there were no exit signs, no flashing lights to point the way, just concave mirrors showing flaws much bigger than they were. I couldn't find deliverance, only different angles of imperfections, some I didn't even know I had until I began looking for them.

I counted each gray hair and line. I decided to just give up.

I sat down and waited for someone to come and rescue me. By now I was drunk, unable to stand from downing the bitter cup of comparison. I sat with my back to the largest image maker, but there was no hiding from myself. No matter where I turned, I was there. There was no escaping me. Those mirrors pleaded.

I writhed in self-pity, unable to run from who I was.

My wails were much louder than I realized. My cry for help was answered. A vibrant woman entered through a door I hadn't seen. First I saw her; then, I saw her everywhere, with the glow of self-assurance infinitely repeated. She was not dazed. She was neither confused nor lost. From the instant she entered, my eyes came off myself and were placed on that exquisite woman who was carrying only a lone, golden, silken sack.

There was something about the way she smiled. Her lips crinkled. Her eyes twinkled. She was more than 30 years my senior, yet in her I saw no flaws. She was older and apparently more wise, because she didn't look in the mirrors, not once.

Her eyes seemed fixed on me.

And with the grace of a swan, she floated over to me and extended her hand. I dropped the baggage I came in with, and without effort I took her hand and rose to her level.

She knew the way out, the unseen door.

I was back in the open air, sitting on a hill, overlooking from where I came. What had occurred? I contemplated what it was like to be lost with nothing but a hideous version of myself.

To my right, I saw her silken sack beside me, and my name was embroidered on it. Inside was everything I wanted to have, do, and become. Then a beautiful voice said, "You're enough, as you are, enough to do whatever your heart desires. You were made for such a time as this. You already have everything you need to fulfill those dreams, whatever they are. Anything you feel compelled to create in your life, you can. The only caveat is that your dream must travel through the hearts of mankind.

That was it! My answer came.

Inside that house of mirrors was an optical illusion. It was not my true self, not what is really there, but a virtual image of what my brain thinks is there. Brains will reflect whatever they are programmed to think. What I speak about myself long enough becomes the dysmorphia I see.

When my eyes are on myself, all seems hopeless. Self-pity ensues and I can't shake that chokehold of depression. But the moment I took my eyes off myself and put them on another, I realized this life was never about me alone.

What I become or achieve cannot be stopped by my inadequacies, but only by what I allow myself to believe.

I found out that I become the most beautiful version of myself when I get down to help another, to lift up someone in need, lead them out of their mess, and walk them towards the light, hand in hand, together.

Work It Out

To exercise your body helps a bit,
But being godly helps a lot.
I use that verse as my excuse to sit
Glued to my desk all day to rot.
Some say a sedentary life is bad;
It has the same effects as smoking.
I'll never make the time to run those laps;
Those stupid studies must be joking.

The temple of the Holy Spirit's us,
So glorify God in your body.
So I assume that means abstain from lust
And hold commands that keep us holy.
Blah, blah, blah, benefits of exercise,
Keeps healthy heart, decreases stress,
Holds back disease, builds up immunities,
Come on! It's looking cute undressed.

I'm told that working out would be a plus,
Yet I don't do it like I should.
It sharpens memory, gains brain proteins;
Endorphins make you feel so good.
And yet I don't recall a single time
Enjoying making myself sweat.
I didn't feel smarter afterwards, more like
I wasted time that I regret.

It fights the age, stops cognitive decline,
Makes dopamine, helps addicts chill.
Anxiety will ease; you can relax;

A workout's like a sleeping pill.
I'm zonked; without the workouts, I can sleep;
I hibernate just on a whim.
If it fights cognitive decline, how come
I lose my keys before I leave the gym?

I'm lazy, yet the Bible seems to hint:
Beloved, I pray that you're in health,
So discipline your shape, so when you preach
You won't disqualify yourself.
Why does it have to be so hard? Can't God
Just blink His eyes and make me fit?
If self-restraint is touted as so great
How come my flesh will not submit?

Present yourself a living sacrifice...
But I'm a burnt-out offering
Not *holy and acceptable to God.*
I wonder if I'm honoring the King.
So getting out of bed each day's a start;
Apparently it's not enough.
I have to make an effort with this bod;
I'll be robust, maybe not buff.

He gives His power to the faint; that's good.
It's only Him who could persuade
Me off my rusty dusty to work out
Since it's been more than a decade.
You won't grow weary when you run, nor faint.
It's Christ whose might will strengthen you.
He makes up for each weakness that I have,
And that's a lot more than a few.

Do not run aimlessly or shadowbox;
Fight faith's good fight; keep up the pace.
You must compete according to the rules
Or be excluded from the race.
I want to live the best life that I can;
Longevity's based on my health.
Just working with no working out is death
And won't bring me a lasting wealth.

So let us lay aside what's our excuse
And with endurance run the race we're in.
Let's sprint so that we may obtain the prize,
For though all run, there's only one who'll win.
Though I may dread my body's training time,
My heart may palpitate and muscles throb,
Sometimes *with fear and trembling* I do quake,
To *work out my salvation* is my job.

Rubbernecking Risk

You are an influential woman;
You shouldn't have to compromise.
Those tempting goodies you've exposed
Are only for your husband's eyes.
To have allure or prove a point,
You need not wear the latest fashion.
For even in a garbage bag
Men's hungry eyes have lusty passion.

That skirt that's just a bit too short
Or outfit painted on too tight
Becomes a rubbernecking risk,
And stopping traffic isn't right.
Hip huggers, slick, with midriff bare
A V-neck top cut far too low;
It doesn't take much skin to show
For pumping blood to start to flow…

Within and out most virile men
The thoughts assaulting come in legions;
Sanguine swords then lead the charge
To treasure trails in rising regions.

If it you've got, then it you flaunt?
Don't buy that lie and show that skin.
If calculated or remiss
You'll aid men's stumble into sin.

I don't suggest thick turtlenecks
On sweltering-hot summer days.
I make the error myself at times,
But doubtless there's another way.
We women are less visual;
It's not the outside that attracts.
We have no clue that we at times
Melt men's resolve like candle wax.

I'm not proposing that we wear
A formless, frumpy, baggy sack,
But be aware of stares we get
From all the fabric that we lack.
So on behalf of all my brothers,
Who fight with might to pass each test,
Please help them with their purity;
Don't leave the house till fully dressed.

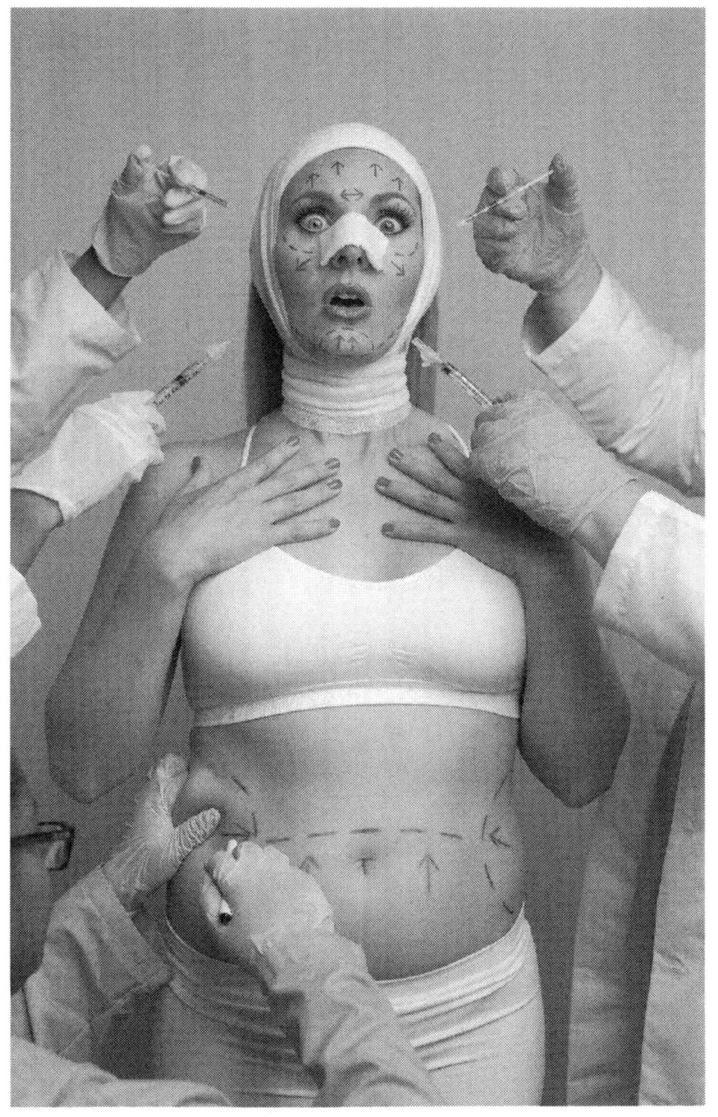

Drastic Plastic Surgery

Like stinging bees, they'll plump your lips,
The fixed look of shock with your brow lift,
Reduce your boobs or blow them up;
You get to pick your size of cup.

They'll pull your neck behind your ears;
And if your head's a balding sphere
Forget toupees, they'll plug in hair.
There's not a part beyond repair.

You can resurface bumps and gunk;
Use dermal fills to raise what's sunk,
They'll suck your flab to make you thin,
They'll change the structure of your chin.

They'll pin those pesky ears right back,
Pull out leg veins so there's no cracks,
They'll take butt fat to fill your cheeks.
An à la carte menu of tweaks.

Penile enlargement can be ensue,
And ladies too can fix hoo-hoo,
A vaginal rejuvenation.
Or, heck, elect to have castration.

Face muscles they will paralyze;
They'll drive up high your droopy thighs.
They'll give that turkey neck a hoist.
Is there anything I haven't voiced?

Insert some pects so you look cut,
A round and high Brazilian butt.
Remove or laser each brown spot;
I'm plastic now; I must be hot!

They'll freeze your fat, remove your tatt,
A narrow nose, and shortened toes,
Shrink cellulite, bleach smile more bright,
They'll tummy tuck; your flab they'll suck.

Remove back teeth for sunken cheeks
Why is your confidence still weak?
When these techniques don't last that long.
You question whether you've been wrong.

You've come unglued, had ribs removed,
You're Vegas-showgirl now approved.
Vacay in Palm Springs to repair.
So why've you fallen to despair?

We're not all shaped like movie stars;
You'll go broke changing who you are.
Conform your form to be like Christ,
Don't try a body-switching heist.

You'll find we're all a corpse that rots;
When buried in an old pine box
Or gold- and diamond-crusted urn.
From dust to dust, we must return.

The you that's real won't be inside
For you have left your earthly hide

The mantel's urn or box in ground,
A lone stark case where you're not found

Don't waste your time and rack your brain
You'll find a glorious new frame,
Your bod from God cannot be topped
Stop putting yours on blocks to chop.

Don't rest your hopes on looking fine,
Old age grabs all, just give it time.
And if immortal spring's your goal
It's best to trim that bloated soul.

Extreme Makeover

We won't believe that we're not up to par
When we discover who we truly are.

Why can't I thrive; what am I doing wrong?
Blend into trends and still I don't belong.
I've worked so hard, and still I'm stuck;
 it's strange.
Is something more extreme in need of change?
'Cause if I change my looks, then doors
 should open?
I've purchased all the products; here's to hopin'!

I'll moisturize my eyes to seal up cracks,
Get beauty sleep, but only on my back.
Slough off the dead and make my skin so soft,
With fresh frocks, all my frumpy fashions doffed.
I rid red eyes by using stinging drops,
And all accessories accent my tops.

I sew in hair or buy the kind that clips;
These Spanx are nice; they squeeze my paunch
 and hips.
My layered base hides well my freckled flaws;
I'm contouring my nose, my cheeks, my jaw.
For cardio, I do the treadmill march,
These stencils used so brows have faultless arch.

With perfect shadow shade, my peepers pop,
Then line and put false lashes on the top.
I pinch my cheeks to find the best of blush,

Then blend pink tones with my kabuki brush.
For pouty lips? Go matte or glossy wet?
And make-up mist ensures my look is set.

Yes, some will lighten skin as I get tan;
I picture photo shoots with blowing fans.
Two-hundred-dollar cuts are held with spray.
I'm going to be somebody soon! Today?
I don't know who I am or where I'll go.
Wrong questions asked with answers
    I don't know.

To fit successful molds, who should I be?
I'm better off a stereotype than me.
I've gained new muscles; my old fat's been lost;
In crisis of identity I'm tossed.
There's something more out there, yes,
    that I know,
But getting there from here, how do I go?

I keep on reaching, but I cannot grasp;
I've talked to everyone. Who's left to ask?
Tried teachers, gurus, all those seminars;
I've called the psychics and they've read my stars.
The question "Who am I?" I'm scared to ask.
What would I look like if I dropped my mask?

To get approval, I've paid through the nose,
Paraded in the Emperor's new clothes.
In vain pursuit, my vision has been skewed,
And all the while I knew not I was nude.

In outward transformation I'm devout,
Yet restoration's best from inside out.

I'd never been more marvelous to see
Than when I let the Lord make over me.
He wipes away false us from beauty bars,
And tells us just exactly who we are.
When we have dropped ourselves
    and put on Him,
We'll shine so bright wherever we are dim.

The quickest way to find out who we are,
Is first to know for sure just *whose* we are.

Perfection Is Delusion

You, as you are, can have it all
Without fixin' or fakin.'
But check your motives; it depends
On what you put your stake in.
When you gaze in the looking glass
Displeased with what you see
Disformity's not truly there;
It's just what you perceive.

God thinks you're beautiful; He'd say,
"Breathgiving in My sight."
It doesn't matter if they say
You're stuffy and uptight.
Like hairs wound on your fretting head
He knows lines on your face,
And He would say be unashamed
For you are saved by grace.

If even truckloads were applied
Of costly wrinkle cream,
One ounce of difference won't be made
Accomplishing your dream.
Don't rate yourself by pin-up girls;
You'll feel intimidated.
God didn't make one size fits all;
It could be you're upgraded.

The beauty industry is fake;
It's only an illusion.
Not happy now? You'll never be;

Perfection is delusion.
'Cause once you find a flaw to fix,
Up pops another one.
If fighting time and gravity
The war is never won.

Become obsessed with losing weight
You're so convinced you gotta.
Can't fit in those designer clothes
But all handbags are Prada.
Yet God's designed a better dress,
Clothing us with righteousness.
These luxury labels leave us less
And will not make us blessed.

And why deprive and starve yourself
Of tasty food to eat?
Enjoy your life, eat, drink, be glad;
You're not here to compete.
Because the good God's got for you
Is meant for you alone.
No one can take it from your grasp,
Not even Barbie's clone.

I know they judge you by your size,
Can't be above an eight.
Wear double digits? Then they eye
What you put on your plate.
We're not cut out of cookie molds;
God made us all unique.
What makes you special, standing out
They say that you should tweak.

The devil wants your focus fixed
On all the lot you're not.
To see you fail, he'll show your flaws;
Don't listen to his plot.
Remember this above all else:
You're made for God's good pleasure.
In that you are incomparable;
He loves you beyond measure.

He'd say, "If you would only trust
In Me, then you would see,
That you've no need to be aware
Of them, but only Me.
Together we'll accomplish all
That's in your heart to do.
I say that you can have your cake
And actually eat it too."

The superficial matters not;
Yes, most can be ignored.
For we can have our heart's desires
If we first seek the Lord.

The After

The Perfect Body

Despite what you see, I've the *perfect body;*
This furrowed *face* did not come gracefully.
I loved and lost and fought so valiantly.
Decrepit is what those short-sighted see.

So listen well, 'though I'm long in the *tooth;*
I've beauty that's renewed by inner youth.
When young at *heart,* it shines to the outside
Like beacons full of wisdom are a guide.

Lined *lips* don't quip when speaking what is good;
These *cheeks* still smile 'though I'm misunderstood.
Dim *eyes* of mine fixed on the good in man;
Creped *neck* still turns to God's eternal plan.

Clothed in compassion, mine's a fashion kind;
A haughty frame of mind you will not find.
A *spine* that's bent, yet stands for what is right;
I use this *body* to give God delight.

My *shoulders* strong to carry heavy yokes,
Inviting *arms* to lift the fallen folks.
Gnarled *fingers* battle, spotted *hands* still war;
I crush my foes, yet comrades are cared for.

These knobby *knees* still bend to pour out prayers.
His Word won't waver; I commit my cares.
A *chest* that pounds to bring about God's will,
Gut feelings warn of sin by turning ill.

On squishy *lap* kids fit to sit and learn;
Legs walked the extra mile without the burn.
And *feet* that went where most would dare not tread,
Away from comfort, spreading truth instead.

Earth Suit Envy

With supermodels I'm obsessed
For they possess je ne sais quoi.
Those walking hangers are so blessed;
Of raw will power I'm in awe.
Like lollipops with bobbing heads,
Crunch celery till I've no mind;
Wish I had haute couture for threads
But that catwalk had left me blind.

Forgot this earth's a pop-up shop,
This garb a temporary tent.
And even if my clothes were swapped,
This coat I wear is just for rent.
Those airbrushed babes are Photoshopped;
I hadn't used my spirit's eyes.
Comparing how my flab does flop,
I pined for cellulite-free thighs.

With cover girls I can't compare
And yet my spouse made no remarks.
He doesn't care what size I wear;
This curvy girl still gives him sparks.
Our faux pas and our overwhelm
Are human; we're judged by appearance.
Aren't we of supernatural realm?
These two confused cause interference.

And ev'n at church my thoughts get caught,
Snagged on regalia, not the higher,
On pastor's dress and not what's taught,

Eyeballing clothes worn by the choir.
Eventually, these shapes will die;
We'll drop this sheath and go on livin'.
Our spirit soon will leap and fly;
That's where attention should be given.

I don't say that it's wrong to mend
An outfit that has wear and tear,
But appliqués and latest trends
Won't really get you anywhere.
Sure, nip and tuck the skin you're in,
But may I say the point is moot?
Too soon it's just a place we've been
Because it's only an earth suit.

Garden of Eatin'

Your body is the temple of God.
Does it need to be cleaned out?

When medical conditions pile,
When wiggling with some extra weight,
When it's been far too long awhile
When we've felt good, forget the great.
When body aches and we're confound,
When joints inflamed scream at us too,
When we've seen doctors all around,
When there is nothing they can do.

Prescriptions swallowed, worn and swigged,
We're leery, popping these horse pills.
Perhaps we are their guinea pigs.
With no results, why get refills?
Remember as a teen we'd sit
On hoods of cars and not make dents?
And now it's just our hats that fit,
For fashion forced to wear those tents!

We know that God's got love for us
But know not how to love ourselves.
We try all that we know and trust
And yet it hasn't helped our health.
Seems everyone has got the key—
"Try this," "Buy this," is their advice.
Organic food, it sure ain't cheap,
And we're not sure it's worth the price.

No counting fat or calories,
No need to weigh or measure food,
Nor spend entire salaries
Removing carbs till we're unglued.
It's simple; take the man-made out
And put the God-made food back in.
The stuff that grows and seeds and sprouts
Is what we humans need to win.

God made what's prime on which to dine;
No other's best on earth to suit.
In Genesis 1:29
He gave herb bearing seeds and fruit.
In perfect bounty's paradise
If we were craving something sweet,
What do you think that we would seize
When it was getting time to eat?

High fructose corn goo for your gut
With additives so artificial
When God has given us a glut
In paradise to whet our whistle?
With every flavor we could try
And boy, it's never been more handy,
Just leave it to the sun to dry
And we have got some Eden candy.

Our body's had enough abuse;
Try produce for superb aminos.
Its protein cells are better used
And plant food's great for your bambinos.

If we crave something savory
Then grab some greens and avocado,
Some wholesome grains to make them flav'ry,
Add endives and a ripe tomato.

Avoid the food devised in labs,
And stick to natural, God-made.
But if our illness can't be beat
Psalm 104:14 our aid.
The Great Physician recommends
That man should be prescribed the herb.
It's right there in His Word, my friend,
So don't blame me if you're perturbed.

Our body's Maker knew for sure;
That's why He made what should go in.
No revolutionary 'cures'
Are miracles to make us thin.
Self-righteous are our habits viewed
'Cause we don't drink, or smoke, do meth.
But we're OD'ing on most foods
And eating to disease and death.

It's not about our girthy waist,
But more our health when grocery shopping.
Can't fill our carts to suit our taste;
Our clothing buttons keep a-popping.
Methinks I've ruined our dinner planned
And most of us don't want to hear it.
Forgive me if I reprimand;
Clean temples better house the Spirit.

Home Repairs

Please plaster over my iniquity;
Seal every hole up in my walls.
Repair the damage, every dent
When earth quick quakes to knock me down.
Make firm foundation solid, strong,
Close open cracks so earth won't rise within.

Treat me, my outer shell so it repels,
Like poison tastes in termites' mouths.
Send forth Your Word to strengthen me;
Support beams sturdy hold the roof,
Secure my shingles to withstand
So when the tempest hits, they will not budge.

Revive my rickety and rundown shack;
Make mighty fortress for the meek
So stricken saints can safely sleep.
Paint my exterior with gold
So passersby decide to look
Inside, and stay, enveloped in Your love.

Beautiful

So stressed and squeezed on every side,
Those grays you hide still scream the story.
Take heart; the Word of God has said
The hoary head is crowned with glory.

You may have circles 'neath your eyes,
And yet they flicker; still, they spark.
They tear up with compassion when
Benevolence has touched your heart.

Your mouth sure has some lines of smiles,
So genuine and freely given,
Affirming to those all around
That God our Gardener has risen.

Your hands, once gorgeous, now well worn
From many years of selfless service.
Don't be ashamed of aging spots;
They're earned; don't let them make you nervous.

Your figure in some people's eyes
May not rate you a perfect ten,
But it reflects the life you've lived,
And all the places you have been.

Like living life unto the full
In celebrations, fellowships;
And loving patiently your kids
Who've caused your grays and spread your hips.

The most beat-up part of your bod,
Dry, cracked, and corned with much abuse,
Will be declared most beautiful
Because those feet had borne Good News.

Beholders see the beauty through the eye,
And God beholds you looking great.
True worth has never been determined by
How briskly you can get a date.

Just as a new-bloomed flower, looks will wilt;
Eventually they all must fade.
And yet that bud was never your best part;
Our spirits flourish, not decay.

For God discovers beauty in our heart,
Not found in symmetry of face.
And there are those most beautiful to Him
Who've lines that cannot be erased.

The seed of beauty ripens best within
A gentle and most kindly spirit.
Indeed, you're truly beautiful, imbued
By God, yet cannot bear to hear it.

Your muscles lose their youthful tone and strength;
Seems every year they do diminish.
But there're still gardens left where you can sow
And keep on reaping 'till you're finished.

Dream Seeds

Do you remember how it used to feel
When you'd play dress-up and it seemed
for real?
You'd change the world with your
divining wand;
When you were that age, it had never dawned—

That you couldn't make it, but folks can be cruel.
Your dreams left fallow as they called you "fool."
You planted precious dreams, seeds in a row.
Where be these buds; how come they
didn't grow?

Did words like weeds from others get involved
And steal nutrition, starving your new bulbs?
They said, "Be practical, and use your head."
So did you shove those dreams
beneath your bed?

You're grown up now, and you don't
feel the same;
It seems like others thrive while you're in pain.
"Forget those dreams; be happy here instead."
When you look too alive, it shows they're dead.

The plans you plant sans water cannot rise.
This is your garden; don't let them sow lies.
Dreams left to rot and now you're not fulfilled,
'Cause you've allowed those seedlings
to be killed.

Do what you've always done; get same results,
Be uninspired in a ho-hum cult.
There's more in you that needs
    to break on through.
Suppress no more! What are you going to do?

You still have time to satisfy that hunger.
"Too late" complaining you wish you
    were younger.
Don't be a people-pleaser; pass the test;
They care, and yet don't always know what's best.

Dust off those dreams you've hidden in your heart;
This season is for nurturing, so start.
Pull out dream weeds; till land; it's not too late.
If you want growth, take time to cultivate.

Replant those seeds and watch how they'll
    take root
From dreams into reality, transmute.
Protect your harvest and don't ever stop
Till every seed becomes a full-grown crop.

Then everything you dreamed you would become
Will be fulfilled by using your green thumb.
And you'll be glad you toiled, and you strove
When dream seeds have become an ample grove.

Also from the Author

Poetic Prescriptions for Pesky Problems

In today's fast-paced, busy life, we are constantly being bombarded with so-called cures for what ails you. Most of these quick fixes are nothing more than mere placebos.

Life on earth can be daunting at times, but there is an accepted "prescription" for the suffering and the challenges of life we face on a daily basis. That prescription can be found in the scriptures—the Word of God.

Poetic Prescriptions for Pesky Problems unleashes these truths in a manner that can be easily understood, with sensitivity and even a bit of irony. It is a prescription that can be taken PRN: whenever necessary!

Katherine's insight and candor is refreshing, and because she goes directly to the heart of the matter, one need not take offense at her right-in-your-face handling of the issue or situation she is confronting, as she points out the way that her Savior has directed her to map out before you in *Poetic Prescriptions for Pesky Problems*.

What people are saying about ***Poetic Prescriptions for Pesky Problems***:

"This chef d'oeuvre is a work of singular, scriptural-linked inspiration...a treasure everyone would enjoy for years to come..."
– D.G. Johnson, PhD

"...[I] highly recommend her anointed book of creative poetry. Her insight, honesty, and truth will minister to you as you enjoy these pages."
– Pastor Desiree Ayres, In His Presence Church, Woodland Hills, CA

"I have yet to find a more beautiful person with such fantastic talent and great love of God...[who] has written a powerful book of such prestigious poetry. One can only be impressed by her accomplishments."
– Ivan S. Markota, Jr., MA, BA, Executive Director Van Mar Academy

"...Her tell-it-like-it-is manner of expressing the issues God puts on her heart can only bless those who 'sup' at this banquet in black and white!"
– Rabbi Anthen Puller, MS.D., CN. PSY., D.D.

"Her words transcended me into an ultimate reality and the realization that I do not walk this life alone. Her refreshing insight and perspective on how life's struggles can be dealt with was so encouraging and admirable. I loved every piece of it.

"Thank you, Katherine, for sharing your work and giving me new hope and unwavering faith in a brighter future. "
– Denver Mendiola

"I thank God for the talent of Katherine Norland! This blessing of a book was just what God ordered and has been the perfect quick pick–me-up on my less-than-stellar days.

"Whoever is thinking about buying this book, I'm writing to tell you what a *tremendous* blessing this book of poetry will be in your life! Every time I open it, God allows me to read just what I need to hear—totally living up to its title.

"Ms. Norland is an extraordinary talent whose compassion, sense of humor, and generosity of spirit leaps off the page.

"Thank you, Ms. Norland!"
– S. Hodge

"Her book is well-organized and divided into categories, making it easy to search out her advice on your particular problem. Easy for anyone of any age to read and understand. Thinking of getting copies for my teenage nieces. Her use of words is creative yet to the point and full of meaning. Her thoughts come through and include instructions from the Bible. Well done, well thought out, creative outlook, put together wonderfully. It's like having her here with you when you need some good advice for things going on in your everyday life. Great to keep out for whenever you need a quick glance to renew your mind and soul. "
– Sara Waterbury

"I received this wonderful book last week. I am a Christian, and in every poem I read, I found a solution for what I'm experiencing in my life. Katherine Norland wrote these poems so that [for] Christian or non-Christian, poet or non-poet, they are enjoyable and carry the message that trusting God for your solutions is the best way. I completely relate to the 'medications' she prescribes in her book. Even as a Christian, I sometimes need a reminder that God is still in charge, and this book of poetry accomplishes that purpose. "
– Michelle Angelini

Poetic Prescriptions for Plaguing Problems: Biblical Remedies for When Life Bites

Does Your Life Bite? You've gone to war in a flypaper dress, trying to catch each buzzing pest: those swarming problems that keep you from living the full life God has for you. Does it seem like your prayers never get answered? Are you wondering where God is in all this? This book of Bible-inspired poetry will assist you in finally terminating those plaguing problems through God's help.

What people are saying about ***Poetic Prescriptions for Plaguing Problems: Biblical Remedies for When Life Bites:***

"It's a powerful and honest book of poetic remedies."

"Katherine Norland has written a powerful, emotional and unapologetically open masterpiece. It is difficult to imagine anyone reading *Poetic Prescriptions for Plaguing Problems* and not having moments of true self-reflection. She provides poetic medication through her reflective and at times blatantly honest review of her own journey through this thing we all call life. Like many other prescription medications, it may not always be easy to swallow her reality pills; however, you will be much better for it in the end. While some may take this book as an opportunity to be judgmental or criticize her openness regarding real-life issues, most will find her particular brand of in-your-face,

reality-based spiritual medication to be just what the doctor ordered to help them get past whatever issues they may be facing and live the life that God truly intended for them to live."
– Wallace Demarria

"A Tour de Force to Challenge Problems"

"I loved everything about this book. Katherine Norland's style of writing is intensely interesting. She attacks life's problems as if she's wearing boxing gloves - SMASH BANG GONE! God is the force in back of her attacks. I related to many of the problems discussed in her poems. There's nothing that says believing in God must be totally serious, and Norland proves this in her poems, since she uses humor. I suffer from chronic pain. One of my favorite stanzas comes from the poem, "All Hell's Come Against Me." The stanza says, "My God won't let me down/Each promise He has kept/He knows the pain I feel/Because He even wept." I'm not alone in my pain, God is right there with me watching over me."
– Michelle Angelini

"A wrecking ball to spiritual strongholds!"

"Metaphors spring to life in lyrical prose exposing our modern-day plagues with an ugly raw truth and guiding us through to see God's grace on the wings of cherubim!"
– Sarah Laurinas-Dolan

"Katherine has a unique style of writing.
In poetic prescriptions for plaguing problems, She is candid, Frank and spot on. She writes from personal experience, so she is very relatable. She does not just present the problem, but always presents the Godly solution so you are always left with hope."
– Nana Stirt

For more information about the author, poetry videos, products, inspirations, and upcoming books, check out:

www.PoeticPrescriptions.com

and

www.KatherineNorland.com

Made in USA - Crawfordsville, IN
23339_9780998395203
04.04.2020 0323